ITALIAN
COOKING

Caroline Manni

Picture credits

Rex Bamber: 29.
Alan Duns: 45.
Melvin Grey: 17.
Christine Hanscomb: 53, 61.
Paul Kemp: 5
David Levin: 21.
Roger Phillips: 9, 25, 37, 41, 49.
Iain Reid: 13, 33, 41, 57.

Edited by Isabel Moore

Produced for K-Mart by

Marshall Cavendish Books Limited
58 Old Compton Street
London W1V 5PA

© Marshall Cavendish Limited 1981

First printing 1981

Printed in Singapore

ISBN 0 85685 964 8

CONTENTS

SOUPS & STARTERS

Minestrone

$\frac{1}{2}$ *cup dried red kidney beans, soaked overnight*
$\frac{1}{4}$ *cup dried chick peas (garbanzos), soaked overnight*
$\frac{3}{4}$ *cup diced salt pork*
$\frac{1}{4}$ *cup olive oil*
2 medium onions, chopped
1 garlic clove, crushed
2 medium potatoes, peeled and diced
4 carrots, cut into $\frac{1}{2}$ in slices
4 celery stalks, cut into $\frac{1}{2}$ in slices
$\frac{1}{2}$ *small head of green cabbage, cored and shredded*
6 tomatoes, skinned, seeded and chopped
5 pints chicken stock
$\frac{3}{4}$ *cup macaroni*

1. Drain the beans and chick peas and put them in a saucepan with fresh cold water. Bring to a boil and simmer for 45 minutes or until they are almost tender. Drain well.

2. Fry the salt pork in a large saucepan until it is crisp and has rendered most of its fat. Remove the dice from the pan.

3. Add the oil to the fat in the pan and heat it. Add the onions and garlic and fry until softened. Stir in the potatoes, carrots and celery and fry for a further 5 minutes, stirring. Add the cabbage and tomatoes and cook for 5 minutes longer.

4. Add the stock, seasoning to taste, beans and chick peas and bring to a boil. Cover and simmer for 35 minutes. Add the macaroni and continue simmering, uncovered, for 10–15 minutes, until the macaroni is *al dente*.

Serves 8

Zuppa alla Pavese

(Bread and egg soup)

---

4 tablespoons butter
4 slices of French or Italian bread
3 tablespoons grated Parmesan cheese
4 eggs
4 cups canned or homemade beef consommé

1. Melt the butter in a skillet. Add the bread slices and fry until they are golden brown on both sides.

2. Place the bread slices in four heated soup bowls and sprinkle with the cheese.

3. Break an egg into each bowl so that it falls to the side of, not on top of, the bread.

4. Bring the consommé to a boil, then ladle it gently over the egg and bread. Serve immediately.

Serves 4

Variation

Zuppa di fontina (Bread and cheese soup): Use 6 tablespoons of butter to fry 12 slices of French or Italian bread until golden brown. Use the slices to line the bottom and sides of an oven-proof soup tureen or casserole. Place a slice of Fontina cheese on each slice of bread. Pour over 6 cups of boiling beef consommé or stock. Put the tureen or casserole in a 350° oven and cook for 10 minutes. Serves 6–8.

Zuppa di Fagioli Fiorentina

(Bean and macaroni soup)

1¼ cups dried white navy beans, soaked overnight
1 cup macaroni pieces
1 lb lean bacon, chopped
1 large onion, grated
2 garlic cloves, crushed
14 oz canned tomatoes
2 quarts light stock or broth
2 tablespoons chopped parsley
grated Parmesan cheese to serve

1. Put all the ingredients, except the parsley, into a saucepan and bring to a boil, stirring frequently, then cover and simmer for 1½–2 hours or until the beans are tender.

2. Add seasoning to taste, then ladle into a warmed tureen. Garnish with the parsley and serve hot, with grated Parmesan cheese.

Serves 6

Insalata di Pomodore e Mozzarella

(Tomato and mozzarella salad)

---

1 lb tomatoes, thinly sliced
½ lb mozzarella cheese, thinly sliced
5 tablespoons olive oil
1 teaspoon dried basil

1. Arrange the tomato slices around the edge of a serving plate. Pile the cheese slices in the center.

2. Mix together the oil, basil and seasoning to taste and pour over the tomatoes. Leave for 5 minutes, then serve.

Serves 4

Variation

Insalata di pomodoro e salami (Tomato and salami salad): Omit the mozzarella cheese and use about 6 oz salami, thinly sliced. Arrange the tomato and salami slices in rows on a serving plate and separate the rows with chopped pitted black (ripe) olives. For the dressing, mix together 6 tablespoons olive oil, 3 tablespoons white wine vinegar, 1 teaspoon lemon juice, 1 crushed garlic clove and seasoning. Pour this dressing over the tomato and salami slices, then chill for 15 minutes. Sprinkle with 1 teaspoon dried basil just before serving. Serves 6.

Bagna Cauda

(Anchovy and garlic dip)

---

8 tablespoons (1 stick) butter
2 tablespoons olive oil
3 garlic cloves, finely chopped
6 anchovy fillets, finely chopped
$\frac{2}{3}$ cup cream
vegetables for dipping (see below)

1. Melt the butter with the oil in a saucepan. Add the garlic and anchovies and cook gently, stirring and mashing with a wooden spoon until the ingredients have almost formed a paste.

2. Stir in the cream and heat through without boiling.

3. Pour the dip into a chafing dish and serve with vegetables for dipping: sticks of carrot, celery and cucumber, cauliflower florets, radishes and green (bell) and red pepper rings.

Serves 4–6

Caponata

(Tangy eggplant appetizer)

---

4 small eggplants, peeled and diced
salt
$\frac{1}{2}$ cup olive oil
4 celery stalks, thinly sliced
2 large onions, thinly sliced
$\frac{1}{2}$ cup tomato paste
$\frac{1}{4}$ cup water
1 tablespoon capers
$\frac{1}{3}$ cup chopped pitted green olives
6 tablespoons red wine vinegar
1 tablespoon sugar

1. Put the eggplants in a colander and sprinkle them with salt. Leave to drain for 30 minutes, then rinse and pat dry with paper towels.

2. Heat all but 2 tablespoons of the oil in a frying pan. Add the eggplant dice and fry until softened and brown. Remove the dice from the pan with a slotted spoon and drain on paper towels.

3. Heat the remaining oil in the pan. Add the celery and onions and fry until lightly browned. Stir in the tomato paste and water. Bring to a boil, then cover and simmer for 15 minutes.

4. Add the capers, olives, vinegar and sugar to the pan and mix well. Stir in the eggplant dice. Continue to simmer gently for 20 minutes, stirring occasionally.

5. Remove from the heat and cool, then chill and serve cold.

Serves 4–6

Fagioli con Tonno

(Bean and tuna salad)

2½ cups dried white navy beans, soaked overnight
2 tablespoons olive oil
1½ teaspoons white wine vinegar
1 teaspoon lemon juice
1 medium onion, finely chopped
1 garlic clove, crushed
1½ teaspoons dried basil
7 oz canned tuna fish, drained and flaked
6 black (ripe) olives, pitted

1. Drain the beans and put them in a saucepan. Cover with fresh cold water and bring to a boil. Simmer for 1–1½ hours or until they are just tender. Drain well and cool.

2. Mix together the oil, vinegar, lemon juice, onion, garlic, basil and seasoning to taste in a salad bowl. Add the beans and stir well to coat with the dressing.

3. Fold in the tuna fish and garnish with the olives.

Serves 4–6

PASTA, PIZZE & RICE
Fettuccine Alfredo

(Noodles with cheese and cream)

---

1 lb fettuccine
4 tablespoons butter
½ cup grated Parmesan cheese
1 cup whipping cream, warmed

1. Cook the fettuccine in boiling water until it is *al dente*. Drain well and tip into a warmed serving bowl.

2. Add the butter, cheese, cream and seasoning to taste and toss well until the butter has melted and all the ingredients are combined. Serve hot.

Serves 4

Spaghetti Vongole

(*Spaghetti with clam sauce*)

---

3 tablespoons olive oil
2 garlic cloves, crushed
1 tablespoon finely chopped capers
1 small onion, chopped
1 lb canned tomatoes, drained
½ teaspoon dried basil
1 lb spaghetti
15 oz canned minced clams, drained
1 tablespoon chopped parsley
lemon wedges to serve

1. Heat the oil in a saucepan and fry the garlic, capers and onion until the onion is softened. Stir in the tomatoes, basil and seasoning to taste, cover and simmer gently for 30 minutes.

2. About 10 minutes before the sauce is ready, cook the spaghetti in boiling water until it is *al dente*.

3. Add the clams and parsley to the tomato sauce and heat through gently, stirring well.

4. Drain the spaghetti and tip it into a warmed serving bowl. Pour over the clam sauce and garnish with lemon wedges.

Serves 4–6

Cannelloni

(Cannelloni with beef and spinach)

---

2 × 14 oz cans tomato sauce
12 cooked cannelloni tubes, kept hot
¼ cup grated Parmesan cheese
Filling
2 tablespoons olive oil
1 small onion, finely chopped
2 garlic cloves, crushed
½ lb ground chuck
10 oz frozen chopped spinach, cooked and drained
1 egg
White sauce
2 tablespoons butter
2 tablespoons flour
1 cup milk

1. To make the filling, heat the oil in a frying pan. Add the onion and garlic and fry until softened. Add the beef and fry until it is browned and crumbly. Remove from the heat. Pour off the excess fat from the pan, then mix in the remaining filling ingredients. Preheat the oven to 375°. Heat the tomato sauce until hot. Stuff the cannelloni tubes with the filling.

2. Now make the white sauce. Melt the butter in a saucepan. Remove from the heat and stir in the flour. Return to the heat and cook for 1 minute, then gradually stir in the milk. Bring to a boil, stirring, and simmer until thickened.

3. Pour about one-third of the tomato sauce over the bottom of a baking dish. Arrange the cannelloni in the dish and cover with the white sauce. Pour over the remaining tomato sauce and sprinkle the cheese on top. Bake for 30 minutes and serve hot.

Serves 4

Lasagne

4 bacon slices, chopped
1 medium onion, finely chopped
1 carrot, finely chopped
$\frac{1}{2}$ lb ground chuck
$\frac{1}{4}$ lb chicken livers, finely chopped (about $\frac{1}{2}$ cup)
$\frac{2}{3}$ cup white wine
1 cup beef stock
$\frac{1}{2}$ lb cooked lasagne, kept hot
$\frac{1}{2}$ lb mozzarella cheese, thinly sliced
$\frac{3}{4}$ cup grated Parmesan cheese
White sauce
2 tablespoons butter
2 tablespoons flour
1 cup milk

1. Fry the bacon in a saucepan until it has rendered its fat. Add the vegetables and beef and fry until browned. Stir in the chicken livers and continue frying for 3 minutes.

2. Stir in the wine, stock and seasoning. Bring to a boil. Cover and simmer for 30–40 minutes or until the sauce is thick.

3. Preheat the oven to 400°. Make the white sauce. Melt the butter in a saucepan. Remove from the heat and stir in the flour. Return to the heat and cook for 1 minute, then gradually stir in the milk. Bring to a boil, stirring, and simmer until thickened.

4. Line a greased baking dish with about one-quarter of the lasagne sheets. Spread over half the meat and cover with half the mozzarella. Top with lasagne sheets then half the white sauce and sprinkle with one-third of the Parmesan. Repeat until the ingredients are used up.

5. Bake for about 30 minutes or until the dish is piping hot.

Serves 4

Risotto Milanese

(Saffron rice)

---

4 tablespoons butter
2 tablespoons chopped beef marrow
1 onion, sliced
2½ cups long-grain or Italian rice
6 tablespoons dry white wine
5 cups boiling beef stock
½ teaspoon crushed saffron threads soaked in 1 tablespoon hot water
½ cup grated Parmesan cheese

1. Melt 3 tablespoons of the butter in a saucepan and fry the marrow and onion until the onion is softened. Add the rice and cook gently, stirring, for 5 minutes.

2. Stir in the wine and about one-third of the stock. Regulate the heat so that the rice is bubbling all the time. Stir occasionally. When the rice swells and the liquid has been absorbed, add another one-third of the stock.

3. Continue cooking, stirring occasionally, until the rice has absorbed all the liquid. Add the remaining stock and cook until the rice is tender and moist.

4. Stir in the saffron, cheese, remaining butter and seasoning to taste and heat through gently, stirring. Serve hot.

Serves 4–6

Risi e Bisi

(Rice with peas)

---

4 bacon slices
4 tablespoons butter
1 onion, thinly sliced
2½ cups long-grain or Italian rice
2 cups shelled fresh peas
6 tablespoons dry white wine
5 cups boiling chicken stock
1 cup grated Parmesan cheese

1. Fry the bacon in a saucepan until it has rendered its fat and is crisp. Remove the bacon from the pan and crumble it.

2. Add 2 tablespoons of the butter to the pan and melt it. Add the onion and fry until softened. Add the rice and peas and cook gently, stirring, for 5 minutes.

3. Stir in the wine and about one-third of the stock. Regulate the heat so that the rice is bubbling all the time. Stir occasionally. When the rice swells and the liquid has been absorbed, add another one-third of the stock.

4. Continue cooking, stirring occasionally, until the rice has absorbed all the liquid. Add the remaining stock and cook until the rice is tender and moist.

5. Stir in the bacon, cheese, remaining butter and seasoning to taste and heat through gently, stirring. Serve hot.

Serves 4–6

Pizza con Pepperoni

(Pepperoni pizzas)

---

6 oz mozzarella cheese, sliced
1 tablespoon chopped parsley
1 pepperoni sausage, thinly sliced
Dough
1 package active dry yeast
$\frac{1}{4}$ teaspoon sugar
$\frac{1}{2}$ cup + 2 tablespoons lukewarm water
2 cups flour
Tomato sauce
2 tablespoons olive oil
1 small onion, finely chopped
1 lb canned tomatoes
$\frac{1}{2}$ cup tomato paste
$\frac{1}{2}$ teaspoon dried basil

1. To make the dough, mix together the yeast, sugar and 2 tablespoons of water. Sift the flour and some salt into a bowl. Add the frothing yeast and the remaining water and mix to make a smooth dough. Knead for 10 minutes or until elastic. Leave to rise for 1 hour or until almost doubled in bulk.

2. Meanwhile, make the tomato sauce. Heat the oil in a saucepan and fry the onion until softened. Stir in the remaining sauce ingredients, cover and simmer for 30 minutes or until thickened.

3. Preheat the oven to 450°. Knead the dough for 3 minutes. Divide in half and roll to $\frac{1}{4}$ in. Place on greased baking sheets.

4. Spread the tomato sauce over the dough, then cover with cheese slices. Sprinkle with the herb and arrange the pepperoni slices on top. Bake for 15–20 minutes or until the crust is crisp.

Serves 2

Pizza Margherita

(*Tomato and cheese pizzas*)

---

6 tomatoes, thinly sliced
6 oz mozzarella cheese, sliced
1 tablespoon dried basil
2 teaspoons olive oil
Dough
1 package active dry yeast
$\frac{1}{4}$ teaspoon sugar
$\frac{1}{2}$ cup + 2 tablespoons lukewarm water
2 cups flour

1. First make the dough. Using a fork, mix together the yeast, sugar and 2 tablespoons of the water. Sift the flour and some salt into a bowl. Add the frothing yeast and the remaining water and mix to make a smooth dough. Knead for 10 minutes until elastic. Leave to rise for 1 hour or until almost doubled in bulk.

2. Preheat the oven to 450°. Knead the dough for 3 minutes. Divide it in half and roll out to $\frac{1}{4}$ in thick. Place on greased baking sheets.

3. Arrange the tomato slices in decorative lines on each dough round and separate them with overlapping cheese slices. Sprinkle over the basil and seasoning to taste, then dribble over the olive oil. Bake for 15–20 minutes or until the crust is crisp.

Serves 2

MEAT & POULTRY

Bistecca a la Fiorentina

(Boiled T-bone steaks, Florence-style)

---

4 T-bone steaks, at least 1 in thick
4 tablespoons butter, cut into dice
4 tablespoons olive oil

1. Preheat the broiler to its highest setting. Arrange the steaks in the broiler and scatter over half the butter dice.

2. Broil for 3 minutes, turn over the steaks and scatter over the remaining dice. Broil for 3 minutes.

3. Reduce the broiler to moderate and cook for a further 3 minutes on each side. This will produce rare steaks: double the cooking time for well done.

4. About 1 minute before the end of the cooking time, rub salt and freshly ground black pepper to taste over the steaks and brush them with the olive oil.

5. Serve hot, with mixed salad and baked potato.

Serves 4

Manzo Stufato

(Beef stew with red wine)

---

2 lb chuck steak, cut into 2 in cubes
1 large onion, sliced
4 bacon slices, chopped
1 cup beef stock
Marinade
1 onion, sliced
3 garlic cloves, sliced
6 peppercorns, lightly crushed
1 bay leaf
1 thyme sprig
1 cup red wine
$\frac{1}{4}$ teaspoon salt

1. Mix together the ingredients for the marinade in a plastic bag. Add the beef cubes. Seal the bag, then marinate in the refrigerator for 5–6 hours or overnight, turning the bag over occasionally.

2. Drain the beef cubes, reserving the marinade. Pat the beef cubes dry with paper towels. Strain the marinade.

3. Fry the onion with the bacon in a Dutch oven until the onion is softened and the bacon has rendered its fat. Add the beef cubes, in batches, and brown on all sides.

4. Stir in the reserved strained marinade and the stock and bring to a boil. Cover tightly and simmer gently for 2 hours or until the meat is tender and the sauce is thick and reduced. Taste and adjust the seasoning before serving.

Serves 4–6

Abbacchio Brodettato

(Lamb with egg sauce)

---

4 tablespoons butter
2 lb boneless lamb (preferably from the leg), cubed
1 small onion, finely chopped
2 garlic cloves, crushed
¾ cup dry white wine
½ cup chicken stock
1 teaspoon dried sage
2 egg yolks
¼ teaspoon grated lemon rind
juice of 2 lemons
parsley sprigs to garnish

1. Melt the butter in a Dutch oven. Add the lamb cubes, in batches, and brown on all sides. Remove the lamb cubes from the pan with a slotted spoon.

2. Add the onion and garlic to the pan and fry until the onion is softened. Stir in the wine, stock, sage and seasoning to taste and bring to a boil.

3. Return the lamb cubes to the pan and stir into the sauce. Cover and simmer for 1½ hours or until the lamb is tender.

4. Lightly beat the egg yolks with the lemon rind and juice and seasoning. Stir about 3 tablespoons of the sauce into the egg yolk mixture, then stir this gently into the sauce in the pan. Cook gently, without boiling, until the sauce has thickened. Serve garnished with parsley sprigs.

Serves 4–6

Costoletta di Maiale alla Milanese

(Breaded pork chops)

---

4 pork chops, trimmed of excess fat
3 tablespoons lemon juice
$\frac{1}{3}$ cup flour
2 eggs
$\frac{2}{3}$ cup fine dry breadcrumbs
$\frac{1}{4}$ cup grated Parmesan cheese
4 tablespoons butter
lemon quarters to garnish

1. Lay the pork chops on a plate in one layer and sprinkle them with the lemon juice. Leave for 10 minutes.

2. Pat the chops dry with paper towels. Mix the flour with seasoning to taste and use to coat the chops.

3. Lightly beat the eggs in a shallow dish. Mix together the breadcrumbs and cheese on a sheet of wax paper. Dip the chops first in the egg, then coat them all over with the crumb mixture. Chill for 15 minutes.

4. Melt the butter in a large frying pan. Add the chops and fry for about 15–20 minutes on each side or until golden brown and cooked through. Serve garnished with lemon quarters.

Serves 4

Costoletta alla Pizzaiola

(Pork chops in tomato and pepper sauce)

---

6 pork chops, about 1 in thick
¼ cup oil
2 garlic cloves, crushed
1½ teaspoons dried basil
⅔ cup red wine
1 lb canned tomatoes, chopped with their juice
3 tablespoons tomato paste
3 tablespoons butter
3 green (bell) peppers, seeded and chopped
1 onion, sliced
½ lb button mushrooms
1½ tablespoons cornstarch dissolved in 2 tablespoons water

1. Rub the chops with salt and pepper. Heat the oil in a large frying pan and fry the chops until they are browned on both sides. Remove from the pan.

2. Pour off all but a thin film of oil from the pan. Add the garlic and herb and stir to mix with the oil. Stir in the wine and bring to a boil. Stir in the tomatoes and tomato paste. Return the chops to the pan and coat with the tomato mixture. Cover and simmer for 40 minutes, basting occasionally.

3. Melt the butter in another frying pan. Add the peppers and onion and fry until softened. Stir in the mushrooms and continue frying for 3 minutes. Stir the vegetables into the pan mixture. Continue cooking, covered, for 15 minutes or until the chops are tender.

4. Transfer the chops to a warmed serving platter. Stir the dissolved cornstarch into the sauce and simmer, stirring, until thickened. Discard the bay leaf and pour over the chops.

Serves 6

Osso Buco

(Stewed veal shank)

¾ cup flour
3 lb veal shank, sawn into 3 in pieces
8 tablespoons (1 stick) butter
1 large onion, sliced
1 lb canned tomatoes
2 tablespoons tomato paste
¾ cup dry white wine
1 teaspoon sugar
Gremolada
1 tablespoon finely grated lemon rind
2 garlic cloves, crushed
2 tablespoons chopped parsley

1. Mix the flour with seasoning to taste and use to coat the veal pieces. Melt the butter in a Dutch oven and fry the veal pieces, in batches, until they are browned on all sides. Remove the veal from the pan.

2. Add the onion to the pan and fry until softened. Stir in the undrained tomatoes, the tomato paste, wine, sugar and seasoning to taste and bring to a boil.

3. Return the veal pieces to the pan. Cover and simmer gently for 1½–2 hours or until the veal is so tender that the meat is almost falling off the bones.

4. Mix together the ingredients for the gremolada and stir into the veal mixture. Cook for a further 1 minute, then serve.

Serves 6

Vitello Tonnato

(Cold veal with tuna sauce)

---

1 × 3 lb boneless veal loin roast
3 garlic cloves, halved
3 anchovy fillets, halved
1 medium onion, sliced
2 carrots, sliced
7 oz canned tuna fish
1¼ cups veal or chicken stock
¾ cup dry white wine
3 tablespoons white wine vinegar
Sauce
½ cup mayonnaise
2 hard-cooked egg yolks, strained
3 tablespoons whipped cream

1. Preheat the oven to 350°. Make six incisions in the meat and insert half a garlic clove and half an anchovy. Place in a flame-proof casserole and add the remaining non-sauce ingredients.

2. Bring to a boil, then cover the casserole tightly and transfer it to the oven. Cook for 1½–1¾ hours or until the veal is tender. Remove from the oven and leave the veal to cool in the liquid.

3. Transfer the veal to a carving board and carve it into thin slices. Arrange these on a large serving platter.

4. Strain the cooking liquid into a bowl. Discard all but 1 cup of the strained liquid, and beat in the mayonnaise, eggs and cream.

5. Pour the sauce over the veal slices to cover them. Chill for 8 hours or overnight. Serve garnished with capers and olives.

Serves 6–8

Scaloppine alla Marsala

(Veal with Marsala)

---

4 veal scallops or scaloppine, pounded thin
3 tablespoons lemon juice
¼ cup flour
5 tablespoons butter
½ cup Marsala

1. Sprinkle the veal with 2 tablespoons of the lemon juice and leave for 30 minutes. Pat dry with paper towels.

2. Season the flour, then use all but 2 teaspoons of the flour to coat the veal.

3. Melt 4 tablespoons of the butter in a skillet. Add the veal and fry for about 4 minutes on each side or until lightly browned. Add the Marsala and remaining lemon juice and continue cooking for 2 minutes.

4. Mix the remaining butter with the reserved flour. Add to the liquid in the pan in small pieces and stir until thickened. Serve hot.

Serves 4

Scaloppine al Limone

(Veal with lemon sauce)

---

4 veal scallops or scaloppine, pounded thin
4 tablespoons lemon juice
5 tablespoons butter
¾ cup dry white wine
2 teaspoons flour
Garnish
lemon slices
chopped parsley

1. Sprinkle the veal with 2 tablespoons of the lemon juice and leave for 30 minutes. Pat dry with paper towels.

2. Melt 4 tablespoons of the butter in a skillet. Add the veal and fry for about 4 minutes on each side or until lightly browned. Remove the veal from the pan and keep hot.

3. Stir the wine and remaining lemon juice into the sediment in the skillet and bring to a boil. Boil for 5 minutes to reduce.

4. Mix the remaining butter with the flour and add to the liquid in the pan in small pieces. Stir until thickened. Add seasoning to taste, then return the veal to the pan. Spoon the sauce over the veal and reheat for 1 minute.

5. Serve garnished with lemon slices and parsley.

Serves 4

Saltimbocca

(Veal with prosciutto and sage)

---

4 veal scallops or scaloppine, pounded thin
2 tablespoons lemon juice
2 teaspoons chopped fresh sage or 1 teaspoon dried sage
4 thin slices of prosciutto
4 tablespoons butter
¼ cup dry white wine

1. Sprinkle the veal with the lemon juice and leave for 30 minutes. Pat dry with paper towels, then rub the veal with half the sage and seasoning to taste. Put a slice of prosciutto on each piece of veal and secure them together with wooden cocktail sticks.

2. Melt the butter in a skillet. Add the remaining sage and stir well into the butter. Add the veal and fry for about 4 minutes on each side.

3. Pour over the wine and cook for a further 2–3 minutes.

4. Remove the cocktail sticks and serve.

Serves 4

(*Top*) Scaloppine al Limone (*Veal with lemon sauce*)
(*Bottom*) Saltimbocca (*Veal with prosciutto and sage*)

Bollito Misto

(Boiled beef, chicken and sausage)

---

1 veal shank
1 × 4 lb·stewing chicken
1 × 1½ lb beef pot roast
6 peppercorns
2 bay leaves
2 teaspoons dried basil
2 leeks, chopped
2 celery stalks, chopped
5 carrots, sliced
12 pearl onions
1 small head of white cabbage, quartered and cored
2 lb potatoes, peeled and sliced
1 Italian boiling sausage

1. Put the veal in a large Dutch oven. Half fill the pan with salted water and bring to a boil, skimming off the scum that rises to the surface. Simmer for 45 minutes. Add the chicken, beef, peppercorns and herbs to the pan. Return to a boil, then cover and simmer for 1½ hours.

2. Add the vegetables and sausage to the pan. Pour in enough water so that the vegetables are nearly covered. Stir well, then continue simmering, uncovered, for a further 1 hour or until all the meats and vegetables are cooked and tender.

3. Discard the veal shank. Remove the chicken, beef and sausage from the pan. Cut up the chicken, slice the beef and cut the sausage into chunks. Arrange the meats on a serving platter.

4. Remove the vegetables from the pan with a slotted spoon and arrange them around the meats. Moisten with a few spoonsful of the stock. Use the remaining stock for soup.

Serves 8–10

Fegato alla Veneziana

(Liver with onions)

---

6 tablespoons olive oil
3 onions, thinly sliced
1 lb calf liver, thinly sliced and cut into 1 × 1½ in strips
lemon quarters to serve

1. Heat the oil in a frying pan. Add the onions and seasoning to taste and stir to mix with the oil. Cover the pan and cook gently for about 30 minutes or until the onions are limp and browned. Stir occasionally. Remove the onions from the pan with a slotted spoon and keep hot.

2. Put the liver strips in the pan and fry briskly for about 1 minute on each side or until they change color.

3. Return the onions to the pan and stir to mix with the liver. Cook for a further 1 minute. Serve with lemon quarters.

Serves 4

Pollo con Peperoni

(Chicken with green pepper)

---

1 large green (bell) pepper, halved and seeded
1 lb canned tomatoes, chopped with their juice
1 onion, thinly sliced
1 garlic clove, crushed
1 chicken bouillon cube
8 large chicken pieces
12 black (ripe) olives, pitted

1. Place the pepper halves in the broiler pan, cut sides down, and broil until the skins are blistered and lightly charred. Peel off the skins, remove the cores and cut the peppers into $\frac{1}{2}$ in wide strips. Alternatively, if you have a gas stove, spear the whole pepper on a long-handled fork and turn it over the flame to char the skin.

2. Put the pepper strips into a Dutch oven and add the tomatoes, onion and garlic. Crumble in the bouillon cube and bring to a boil, stirring.

3. Rub the chicken pieces with seasoning and place them in the pan, skin side down. Spoon the sauce over them. Cover tightly and simmer gently for 30–40 minutes, basting occasionally.

4. Lift the chicken pieces onto a warmed serving plate and keep hot. Stir the olives into the sauce, and taste and adjust the seasoning. Pour the sauce over the chicken.

Serves 4

(Top) Pollo con Peperoni *(Chicken with green pepper)*
(Bottom) Pollo alla Milanese *(Chicken with ham and cheese)*

Pollo alla Milanese

(Chicken with ham and cheese)

---

4 chicken breasts, skinned and boned
4 slices of ham
2 tomatoes, skinned and sliced
⅓ cup grated Parmesan cheese
Marinade
2 tablespoons oil
2 tablespoons lemon juice

1. Place the chicken breasts between two sheets of wax paper and pound with a rolling pin or meat mallet until they are flattened.

2. Arrange the chicken breasts, in one layer, in a baking dish. Mix together the ingredients for the marinade and pour over the chicken. Turn them to coat, then marinate in the refrigerator for 2 hours.

3. Preheat the oven to 300°. Place a slice of ham on each chicken breast and cover with tomato slices. Sprinkle with half the cheese.

4. Cover the dish with foil and bake for 40 minutes. Uncover and sprinkle over the remaining cheese. Increase the oven temperature to 450° and move the dish to the top of the oven. Continue cooking until the cheese on top is lightly browned.

Serves 4

Petti di Pollo alla Valdostana

(Chicken breasts with mushrooms and cheese)

---

4 chicken breasts, boned
3 tablespoons flour
5 tablespoons butter
¼ cup olive oil
1 cup thinly sliced tiny button mushrooms
½ lb mozzarella cheese, thinly sliced
½ cup white wine
⅓ cup chicken stock

1. Place the chicken breasts between two sheets of wax paper and pound with a rolling pin or meat mallet until they are flattened. Coat the chicken breasts with the flour.

2. Melt 4 tablespoons of the butter with the oil in a skillet. Add the chicken breasts and fry for 3–4 minutes on each side or until browned and cooked through. Transfer the chicken breasts to a warmed, flameproof serving dish. Sprinkle them with salt and pepper and keep hot. Preheat the broiler.

3. Add the mushrooms to the skillet and cook for 2 minutes or until barely tender. Spread the mushrooms over the chicken breasts, then cover with the cheese slices.

4. Pour the wine and stock into the skillet and bring to a boil, stirring well. Simmer for 10 minutes or until the liquid becomes slightly syrupy.

5. Meanwhile, place the chicken under the broiler and cook until the cheese melts and begins to brown.

6. Season the sauce in the skillet and stir in the remaining butter. Pour the sauce around the chicken in the dish and serve.

Serves 4

Pollo alla Cacciatora

(Chicken with wine, tomatoes and mushrooms)

1½ tablespoons butter
2 tablespoons olive oil
2 garlic cloves, crushed
2 scallions or green onions, finely chopped
1½ cups sliced mushrooms
8 chicken pieces
¾ cup dry white wine
¼ cup chicken stock
6 tomatoes, skinned, seeded and chopped
1 bay leaf
½ teaspoon flour
chopped parsley to garnish

1. Melt 1 tablespoon of the butter with the oil in a Dutch oven and fry the garlic and scallions until softened. Stir in the mushrooms and fry for a further 2 minutes. Remove the vegetables from the pan with a slotted spoon.

2. Add the chicken pieces to the pan and brown on all sides. Return the vegetables to the pan and add the wine, stock, tomatoes, bay leaf and seasoning to taste. Bring to a boil, then cover and simmer for 40 minutes or until the chicken is cooked.

3. Lift out the chicken pieces and keep them hot on a serving plate. Boil the sauce to reduce it slightly.

4. Mix the remaining butter with the flour and add to the sauce in small pieces. Stir until thickened. Discard the bay leaf, and taste and adjust the seasoning. Pour the sauce over the chicken and sprinkle with chopped parsley.

Serves 4

FISH & VEGETABLES

Trote Marinate

(Trout marinated in vermouth)

6 small trout, cleaned
$\frac{1}{4}$ cup flour
4–6 tablespoons oil
Marinade
$\frac{1}{2}$ cup oil
2 onions, sliced
2 garlic cloves, sliced
3 tablespoons white wine vinegar
$\frac{1}{3}$ cup dry vermouth
2 strips of lemon rind
2–3 sage leaves
1 rosemary sprig
8 peppercorns

1. Coat the trout with the flour. Heat the oil in a skillet and fry the trout, in batches, for about 5 minutes on each side or until they are golden and just cooked through. Remove from the pan and arrange, in one layer, in an earthenware dish.

2. For the marinade, heat the oil in a saucepan and fry the onions and garlic until softened. Stir in the remaining marinade ingredients and bring to a boil.

3. Pour the boiling marinade over the trout and cool. Marinate in the refrigerator for at least 3 days, turning the trout from time to time.

Serves 6

Cacciucco

(Seafood stew)

$\frac{1}{4}$ cup olive oil
2 garlic cloves, chopped
1 fresh red chili pepper, seeded and chopped
$\frac{3}{4}$ lb raw shrimp, shelled, deveined and chopped
$\frac{1}{2}$ lb squid, skinned, cleaned and chopped
$\frac{1}{2}$ cup dry white wine
3 tablespoons tomato paste
2 cups water
$\frac{1}{2}$ lb cod fillets, chopped
$\frac{1}{2}$ lb haddock fillets, chopped
To serve
4 slices of Italian bread, toasted
1 garlic clove, halved
2 tablespoons chopped canned pimiento

1. Heat the oil in a Dutch oven and fry the garlic and chili pepper for 5 minutes. Stir in the shrimp and squid. Cover and cook gently for 30 minutes. Stir in the wine and continue cooking, uncovered, for 15 minutes.

2. Add the tomato paste, water and seasoning to taste, and stir well. Bring to a boil. Add the cod and haddock pieces. Cover the pan again and simmer for 15 minutes.

3. Rub the bread slices on both sides with the garlic halves, then discard the garlic. Place a slice of bread in each of four soup bowls.

4. Ladle the stew over the bread and garnish with the pimiento.

Serves 4

Insalata di Mare

(Seafood salad)

---

6 tablespoons olive oil
3 dozen mussels, scrubbed
2 cups water
8–10 baby squid, tentacles cut from the bodies
2½ lb raw shrimp
1 tablespoon lemon juice
½ dried red chili pepper, finely flaked
2 tablespoons chopped parsley

1. Heat 2 tablespoons of the oil in a saucepan. Add the mussels and cover tightly. Shake the mussels over the heat until they open. Remove the mussels from their shells, reserving the liquid, and place them in a shallow serving dish. Discard any where the shells do not open.

2. Put the mussel liquid back into the saucepan and add the water and squid pieces. Bring to a boil and simmer for about 20 minutes or until the squid are tender (this varies according to their size). Add the shrimp and cook for 10 minutes longer.

3. Drain the squid and shrimp and cool. Cut the squid bodies into rings and add with the tentacles to the mussels. Shell and devein the shrimp and add to the mussels.

4. Mix the remaining olive oil with the lemon juice, chili pepper and a pinch of salt. Stir this dressing into the seafood. Sprinkle the parsley and a little pepper on top and chill for 2 hours before serving.

Serves 6

Fritto Misto di Mare

(Deep-fried fish and shellfish)

---

oil for deep frying
2 flounder fillets, skinned and cut into 1 in strips
2 whitefish fillets, skinned and cut into 1 in strips
4 scallops
$\frac{3}{4}$ lb jumbo shrimp, shelled (but tails left on) and deveined
lemon wedges to serve
parsley sprigs to garnish
Batter
1 cup flour
$\frac{1}{4}$ teaspoon salt
1 egg, separated
1 tablespoon oil
1 cup milk
1 egg white

1. First make the batter. Sift the flour and salt into a bowl. Add the egg yolk and oil and mix well. Gradually beat in the milk to make a smooth batter. Beat the 2 egg whites until stiff and fold into the batter.

2. Heat the oil in a deep fat fryer to 375°.

3. Coat the pieces of fish with the batter and deep fry, in batches, for 3–4 minutes or until crisp and golden brown. Drain on paper towels.

4. Serve hot with lemon wedges, garnished with parsley sprigs.

Serves 4–6

Peperonata

(Red peppers with tomatoes)

---

2 tablespoons butter
2 tablespoons olive oil
1 large onion, sliced
1 garlic clove, crushed
1 lb sweet red peppers, seeded and cut into strips
1 lb tomatoes, skinned and chopped
1 bay leaf

1. Melt the butter with the oil in a saucepan and fry the onion and garlic until softened. Stir in the peppers. Cover the pan and cook gently for 15 minutes.

2. Add the tomatoes, bay leaf and seasoning to taste and mix well. Continue cooking, uncovered, for a further 20 minutes. Discard the bay leaf before serving, hot or cold.

Serves 4–6

DESSERTS

Zuccotto

(Cream and cake dessert)

$2\frac{1}{2}$ *cups whipping cream*
$\frac{1}{4}$ *cup + 2 tablespoons confectioners' sugar, sifted*
$\frac{1}{2}$ *cup filberts, toasted*
$\frac{1}{2}$ *lb fresh cherries, halved and pitted*
$\frac{1}{4}$ *lb dark sweet chocolate, grated*
$\frac{1}{4}$ *cup brandy*
$\frac{1}{4}$ *cup orange liqueur*
2×8 *in chocolate cake layers, each sliced into 2 layers*
2 tablespoons unsweetened cocoa powder

1. Whip the cream with the $\frac{1}{4}$ cup sugar until thick. Fold in the filberts, cherries and chocolate. Chill.

2. Mix together the brandy and liqueur.

3. Line the bottom and sides of a 1 quart capacity round deep mold with three of the cake layers, cutting the cake into pieces so it will fit. Sprinkle the cake with the brandy mixture.

4. Spoon the cream mixture into the cake-lined mold and cover with the remaining cake layer. Chill for 2 hours.

5. Unmold the dessert onto a serving plate. Mark it into quarters and sprinkle alternate quarters with the remaining sugar and the cocoa powder.

Serves 8–10

Ciliege al Marsala

(Cherries in Marsala)

---

2 lb canned Morello or Bing cherries, drained and pitted
⅔ cup Marsala
½ teaspoon grated nutmeg
1 tablespoon sugar
whipped cream to serve

1. Put the cherries, Marsala, nutmeg and sugar into a saucepan and bring to a boil, stirring to dissolve the sugar. Simmer gently for 10 minutes.

2. Lift out the cherries with a slotted spoon and pile them in a serving bowl.

3. Boil the Marsala for 3–4 minutes to reduce, then pour over the cherries. Cool and chill for 1 hour. Serve topped with whipped cream.

Serves 4

Zuppa Inglese

(English 'soup' or trifle)

⅔ cup candied fruit, chopped if necessary
2 tablespoons brandy
3 tablespoons cornstarch
⅔ cup sugar
1¾ cups milk
6 egg yolks, lightly beaten
1 teaspoon vanilla extract
1 cup whipped cream
½ cup rum
2 × 7 in white cake layers, each sliced into 2 layers
3 egg whites
¾ cup superfine sugar

1. Mix the fruit with the brandy and leave for 1 hour. Put the cornstarch and sugar into a saucepan and stir in 1½ cups of the milk. Cook gently, stirring, until thick and smooth.

2. Mix together the egg yolks and remaining milk. Gradually stir in the thickened custard, then return to the pan. Cook gently, stirring, until very thick. Stir in the vanilla. Cool, then chill for 1 hour. Preheat the oven to 450°. Fold the cream into the custard.

3. Sprinkle the rum over the cake layers. Sandwich together the layers with the custard and place the assembled cake on a greased baking sheet. Spread the fruit and brandy mixture over the top.

4. Beat the egg whites until frothy, then gradually beat in the sugar. Continue beating until the meringue will stand in a stiff peak. Spread over the top and sides of the cake to cover. Bake for 4–5 minutes or until the meringue is lightly browned.

Serves 6

Cassata alla Siciliana

(Ice cream mold)

---

1 pint vanilla ice cream, softened
½ pint chocolate ice cream, softened
⅔ cup whipping cream
½ cup confectioners' sugar
⅔ cup finely chopped mixed candied fruits
1 egg white

1. Use a metal spoon dipped in hot water to spread the vanilla ice cream over the bottom and sides of a 1½ quart freezerproof mold. Freeze until solid.

2. Cover the vanilla ice cream with a layer of chocolate ice cream, leaving a well in the center for the filling. Freeze again until solid.

3. Whip the cream with the sugar until thick. Fold in the fruit. Beat the egg white until stiff and fold into the cream mixture. Spoon this filling into the well in the ice cream-lined mold. Tap the mold to release any air bubbles. Smooth the top and cover with foil. Freeze until firm.

4. Dip the mold quickly into hot water and unmold the cassata onto a plate. Serve cut into wedges.

Serves 8

Zabaione

(Zabaglione)

---

4 egg yolks
¼ cup sugar
½ cup Marsala

1. Put the egg yolks and sugar in the top of a double boiler, away from the heat, and beat until they turn thick and creamy.

2. Place over the bottom pan containing hot just simmering water. Add the Marsala and continue beating until the mixture becomes a creamy, thick amber foam. Serve immediately.

Serves 4

Crostata di Ricotta

(Cheesecake)

---

2 cups flour
12 tablespoons (1½ sticks) butter, cut into small pieces
4 egg yolks, lightly beaten
2 tablespoons sugar
5 tablespoons Marsala
1½ teaspoons grated lemon rind
Filling
2¼ lb (5 cups) ricotta cheese
½ cup sugar
2 tablespoons flour
½ teaspoon vanilla extract
grated rind and juice of 2 lemons
3 tablespoons raisins
2 tablespoons slivered almonds
1 egg white, lightly beaten

1. Sift the flour and some salt into a bowl and make a well in the center. Add the butter, egg yolks, sugar, Marsala and lemon rind and combine. Knead the dough until it is smooth and will form a ball, but do not overhandle it. Chill for 1 hour.

2. Preheat the oven to 350°. Roll out about three-quarters of the dough and use to line a greased 9 in springform pan.

3. For the filling, beat the cheese with the sugar, flour, vanilla, lemon rind and juice and raisins. Spoon into the pie shell and smooth the top. Sprinkle over the almonds.

4. Roll out the remaining dough and cut it into long strips. Lay in a lattice pattern over the filling. Brush with the egg white. Bake for 1 hour or until the pastry is golden brown and the filling is firm to the touch. Cool before serving.

Serves 6–8

INDEX